marriage

A teaching document from the
House of Bishops of the Church of England

ISBN: 0 7151 3829 4
Published in 1999 for the House of Bishops of the General Synod of the
Church of England by Church House Publishing

Copyright © The Archbishops' Council 1999

All rights reserved. Parishes, benefices, team and group ministries, diocesan bodies, charitable organizations, governmental and non-governmental organizations, and Churches of the wider Christian community have permission to reproduce this booklet in part or in its entirety for local use, provided the copies include the above copyright notice and no charge is made for them. Any other reproductions, storage or transmission of material from this publication by any other means or in any form, electronic or mechanical, including photocopying, recording, or any information storage and retrieval system, requires prior written permission from the Copyright and Contracts Administrator, The Archbishops' Council, Church House, Great Smith Street, London SW1P 3NZ (Tel: 020 7898 1557; Fax: 020 7898 1449; email: copyright@c-of-e.org.uk).

Printed by ArklePrint Ltd, Northampton
Designed by Jordan Design

contents

Preface by the Archbishops of Canterbury and York	5
Why is marriage important?	7
What are the challenges facing those who approach marriage?	10
How is Christian marriage distinctive?	12
How does the Church understand marriage breakdown?	14
Does the Church believe that a further marriage is possible after divorce?	17
How do we know God in marriage and marriage breakdown?	19
Appendix 1: What does the Church have to say to a couple who are living together without being married?	21
Appendix 2: What does the Church have to say to someone whose marriage has broken down?	23

preface

It has always been the Church's mission to proclaim the unchanging gospel to the changing world. Lifelong marriage itself represents an unchanging ideal, and one which is the bedrock of a rapidly changing society. The House of Bishops considers it timely on the eve of the new millennium to reaffirm the Church of England's teaching on marriage. We have sought to relate this teaching to the pastoral needs of people in our communities today, so that they might approach marriage with confidence.

We pray that this statement will be used as a stimulus to commend the gift of marriage to people in our land, and as a basis for teaching in our parishes.

On behalf of the House of Bishops:

George Cantuar
20 September 1999

David Ebor

why is marriage important?

God is love *(1 John 4.16)*, and in creating human beings he has called us to love, both himself and one another. The love of God the Father for his Son is the ground of all human love, and through the Holy Spirit we may dwell in that love, which the Son has shown to us *(John 15.9)*. Marriage is a pattern that God has given in creation, deeply rooted in our social instincts, through which a man and a woman may learn love together over the course of their lives. We marry not only because we love, but to be helped to love. Without the practice and disciplines of marriage, our love will be exhausted and fail us, perhaps very harmfully to ourselves and others. When publicly and lawfully we enter into marriage, we commit ourselves to live and grow together in this love.

Marriage is not, of course, the only pattern that is given us for a life of love. Unmarried people, of whom Jesus himself was one, have a different pattern of loving relationships, also to be valued and appreciated. Such people also have a special place in the life of the Church, since they have often made a decisive contribution by being available for initiatives in ministry. Married people, too, love others than their partners: they love their children, friends, strangers, and even their enemies *(cf. Mt 5.44)*. But their marriage is the central focus of their relationships, around which other relationships grow; their home life together is their primary

why is marriage important?

contribution to society. Sexual intercourse, as an expression of faithful intimacy, properly belongs within marriage exclusively. The three blessings that belong to marriage are traditionally described as the procreation and nurture of children, the hallowing and right direction of natural instincts and affections, and the mutual society, help and comfort which each affords the other in prosperity and adversity.

Through marriage each of the partners grows in maturity, and is helped to overcome personal failings and inadequacies. It is a school of patience and forgiveness. By it a new unit of society is created: a couple, stronger than the sum of its members, held together by the bond of domestic friendship. Together the couple can extend love to other people: to their own children, in the first instance, who belong naturally within their domestic circle; and not only to them, but to many others who interact with them in a variety of ways. Their love enables them to make a strong contribution to society so that the weakening of marriage has serious implications for the mutual belonging and care that is exercised within the community at large.

why is marriage important?

Love has many aspects. It includes the fascination that draws us to those with whom we resonate and whom we find exciting. It includes the sense of loyalty we feel to those who are 'our own', members of our family or community. It includes the willingness to sacrifice ourselves for others' welfare; and it includes the respectful appreciation of another's qualities and gifts which makes close cooperation possible. It is not a mistake that all these different things are summed up by the one word 'love', for a deep and growing love includes them all in different measures at different times. For love in marriage to grow, it must develop not along one of these fronts only, but now along one, now along another. The emotional failure of a marriage may indicate that one or both partners have not recognized the need for growth, and are looking simply to repeat the same kind of emotional satisfactions with which their love began.

what are the challenges facing those who approach marriage?

There is a great deal in our culture which discourages us from making binding and public promises. That is undoubtedly a difficult thing to do, and requires courage. But the promises are an important part of entering marriage. If love is to grow, it needs an explicit commitment of the couple to stay with each other through changing circumstances, through personal development and growth, and through the process of growing older and approaching death. Making promises 'before God and in the face of this congregation' declares our conscious willingness to view love not merely as a comfort, but as a lifelong responsibility.

But the promises are also liberating. Through them we focus our intentions, and offer one another a shared future in a way that we could hardly dare to do otherwise. By making our promises in public, we call on a community of well-wishers to support us in our resolve to be a couple, an important assistance in a culture that is generally unsupportive to any kind of commitment. And by making our promises before God in a setting of prayer, and listening to his promises to us, we can be assured of his faithful love to sustain our own weak resolve to be faithful.

what are the challenges facing those who approach marriage?

Approaching marriage requires realism and self-awareness. In deciding to marry, a couple needs to consider what will be demanded by the tasks of parenthood and mutual support, and what the implications may be for the career of each. Nobody can enter through this door without closing others, and unresolved ambivalence may be the root of problems that develop later. In a society which inculcates a false idea of freedom as lack of attachment, and fosters all kinds of misleading fantasies about sex, the growth of a relationship towards marriage is often, and very understandably, surrounded by hesitation and anxiety. The social and emotional steps by which couples come to enter marriage are often complicated, and some finally think about lifelong commitment only when they are already living together. This route of approaching marriage is exposed to uncertainties and tensions and is not to be recommended. But it was not uncommon in earlier periods of history, and the important thing is simply that the point of commitment should be reached.

how is Christian marriage distinctive?

Marriage is a gift of God in creation; and the marriage of unbelievers is as real, and often as enduring, as the marriage of believers. The words 'till death us do part' are not a special religious ideal; they describe the form of relationship that God has given to human beings as a natural endowment. Knowing that they must both one day die, the partners offer each other a security and continuity in life, that will help them to approach death with humility and a good conscience. Yet it is important that those who marry know the full extent of what they are doing. And Christians believe that that requires an understanding of the love that God has shown mankind in Christ, a love which marriage is called to reflect. Those who understand God's love to them will understand their own love as a part of God's work in the world, and will be better equipped for what they undertake. Precisely because it is a lifelong partnership, marriage is chosen by God to express the permanence of his love for us, which accompanies us through all the changing scenes of life not only until the day we die, but beyond death to resurrection.

how is Christian marriage distinctive?

The description of Christian marriage as a 'sacrament' is valued because it has its source in the New Testament (the 'great mystery' of *Eph 5.32*), although the term does not have exactly the same sense as when it is applied to the two 'sacraments of the Gospel', baptism and eucharist. It means that the pledged relation of husband and wife is a sign of the pledge of love that Christ has for his Church, the promises he has made to it, the faithfulness, forgiveness, and patience that he has shown it, the delight he takes in it.

The grace of God in the Holy Spirit is given to all who enter marriage in the conscious desire to hear his call, seeking his strength to live together as they have promised. This is why marriage in the context of worship, properly prepared for by a process of reflection and discussion about the life of faith, is an important ministry of the Church.

how does the Church understand marriage breakdown?

Marriage, implying as it does a lifelong horizon, is violently cut short and frustrated when a couple separate from each other short of death. Those who have suffered this sad experience can attest to the emotional scars that it inflicts, and there is plentiful evidence of the hurt done to others, especially to children of the broken marriage.

Sometimes a marriage never appears to have been 'real', perhaps because one or both of the partners was unfit for marriage psychologically or physically, or too immature to make the promises in full understanding. However, it is only in very restricted circumstances that the secular courts can annul such marriages, and in any event they do not account for more than a tiny fraction of marriages that break down today. In most cases we have to acknowledge that a real marriage, in every sense, begun with real hope and expectation, has come to grief.

All Christians believe that marriage is 'indissoluble' in the sense that the promises are made unconditionally for life. 'For better for worse, for richer for poorer, in sickness and in health, to love and to cherish, till death us do part, according to God's holy ordinance': these well-known words, used for many centuries, are decisive for what it means to undertake marriage. Some strands of the Western Church have concluded from this that a divorce decree is ineffective and a subsequent marriage invalid in the eyes of God. The reformers of the Church of England did not believe that this was taught in Scripture, and they did not teach it in *The Book of Common Prayer*. In this respect they came closer to the understanding of the Eastern Church, which allows for the possibility of the 'death' of a marriage. Yet from the seventeenth century until the present century English Church law made no allowance for a second marriage in the lifetime of a previous partner; and some Anglican Christians have believed, and still do, that such a marriage is, strictly speaking, impossible. These convictions demand respect, though they are not those of the Church of England as a whole. And they emphasize one aspect of the truth which we all acknowledge: a broken marriage can never put us back where we were before; it leaves relational ties and obligations behind which do not disappear — to the children of the marriage, to the former partner, and to his or her parents, relatives and friends.

The disaster of a broken marriage is not simply the result of chance or accident. Promises have been broken in attitudes the partners have taken and in ways they have treated each other. Marriage breakdown is the fruit of lovelessness and carelessness, but not only of the partners; others share the responsibility for it. Contemporary society imposes heavy pressures on marriage. The quest for individual self fulfilment can undermine the commitment that marriage entails. Disappointments and demands in the world of work, and the anxieties of bringing up children may make it much more difficult for a couple to maintain a good understanding with each other. The ease of legal divorce itself may be a destructive factor. The principle of the law is that a divorce occurs only when the marriage has already broken down; but in practice the law as it stands does not always encourage those facing marriage difficulties to work them through.

Everything that contributes to the breakdown of a marriage offends against God's love. It harms the community as a whole, and quite specifically harms the partners and their children. But it is unwise, and may also be uncharitable, for those outside the marriage to attempt to say precisely where the fault lies in any case. Should domestic violence and abuse take place, the Church must condemn it frankly, and offer appropriate support to its victims. At deeper levels of responsibility for breakdown, however, the Church is not interested in assigning blame to one partner or the other but in helping people accept responsibility for what they have done. Partners to a broken marriage need to search themselves honestly, and to overcome the temptation of always blaming each other, the circumstances, and so on. At the heart of the gospel is a warning against self-justification; we need this warning especially when we are trying to cope with the sense of shame and humiliation which is almost inseparable from the experience of marriage breakdown.

does the Church believe that a further marriage is possible after divorce?

In some circumstances to marry again after divorce may compound the wrong that one has done, e.g. when obligations to the partner or children of the first marriage are not being met; or when the marriage causes further hurt to the children of the previous one; or when an act of unfaithfulness which contributed to the breakdown is the basis of the new relationship. It may sometimes be a sign of emotional immaturity; and it may also be imprudent, emotionally and financially. In other circumstances, on the other hand, it may be responsible, prudent (e.g. in relation to the care of young children) and emotionally wise. There is no simple rule for discerning this, for each case is different. But the Church has learned to stress the importance of putting a clear distance between a new marriage and the old: a distance of time, of local setting, and of relationship. Time is needed to recover emotional stability and good judgement; a new setting is needed, where the former partner is not forced to endure the reopening of old wounds; and a new relationship is needed, avoiding suspicion that the new marriage consecrates an old infidelity.

In this situation it is for the partners, whatever advice they take, to decide whether to marry. But it is not only for the partners, but for the Church itself, to decide whether the marriage ought to be witnessed and solemnized in an act of worship. The Church has a responsibility to safeguard the understanding of marriage as a

does the Church believe that a further marriage is possible after divorce?

lifelong vocation. In the past the Church of England has sought to meet this responsibility by refusing to have the marriage of a person with a previous partner living solemnized in church. In this way it has tried to indicate clearly that the breach of a marriage is so serious a matter that entering a second one is not something which anybody can claim as a right. When a Christian in this situation has judged it appropriate to marry again, the Church has been willing to respect that decision and to pray with the couple; but it has not been willing to solemnize the marriage.

For some time, now, the Church of England has been discussing changes to this policy in response to changing pastoral needs, and a number of dioceses have drawn up experimental guidelines for alternative practices. Should the Church as a whole decide upon an alternative, it will be on precisely the same principles that have guided it up to this point: that marriage is an unconditional commitment for life; that a further marriage after a divorce is an exceptional act; that it must be approached with great honesty and circumspection; and that the Church itself, through its ministry, has a part in deciding whether or not a marriage in such circumstances should take place in the context of church worship.

how do we know God in marriage and marriage breakdown?

Marriage is an unparalleled turning-point in anybody's life; the troubles surrounding the breakdown of marriage are a low point, often as terrible as bereavement itself. The Church is glad to support people at these critical moments, joyful or tragic. But it wants them to discover the opportunity that the moment contains: an opportunity to know God, and to realize the purposes that he has for their lives. God often meets us when we come to the edge of own capacities and stand on the brink of unknown possibilities and dangers. He meets us as free and generous mercy, and as demanding holiness; these two characteristics are not in tension or contradiction, but complementary. The scope of God's holiness is the scope of his mercy, and the more we are ready to open ourselves to the demand, the more we will know of his generosity, forgiving us where we have failed and granting us success where we thought we were bound to fail. The reason that the Church continues to insist on the highest expectations of married couples, when so many of our contemporaries are content to treat the matter lightly, is that much more than marriage is lost if we let the scope of the demand and generosity of God slip from our sight. But if we respond to them seriously, we are changed by them; and our lives acquire hopefulness and patience in the knowledge of his love.

Appendix 1

what does the Church have to say to a couple who are living together without being married?

The relationships of couples who live together without being married are of many different kinds. Some are short term and experimental; some have serious long-term hopes; some are already stable and enduring. Sometimes a couple intends marriage in the future; sometimes they feel negatively about it, either because of personal insecurities or disappointments which they have brought from the past, or from a suspicion, which our culture tends to reinforce, of formal and binding ties. Some couples agree on what their expectations are; some cannot discuss them freely together, so that each is uncertain of what the other has in mind.

Whatever may be your case, the Church would like to help you address and resolve any questions there may be in your mind about your relationship, which may become a source of grave anxiety if they are not addressed. If you wish to discuss these questions without prejudice, the Church's ministers will be glad to talk in confidence with you, as a couple or individually, and, if you wish, to pray with you informally that God will show you his will for your future.

Appendix 1

But it may be, in fact, that you have resolved the question of your future between yourselves already, that you are quite certain of your lasting commitment to each other, and are living naturally together among your friends as husband and wife. Even so, the Church would encourage you to make the public stand that is implied in your way of life, expressing your promises to one another and praying together, as others pray with you, for God's assistance.

In any case, the strength of your relationship and its potential for service to the community depend upon your enjoying a full and confident relationship with God and his people. The worshipping community, which is ready to welcome you in celebrating and learning of God's love, is the proper supportive context for the personal relationship at the centre of your life to flourish.

Appendix 2

what does the Church have to say to someone whose marriage has broken down?

The Church will do whatever it can to help you to put past failures behind you, and to claim the free forgiveness that Christ has won for all our sins, small and great. Freedom of conscience and a joyful confidence, which is neither afraid of the past nor haunted by it, is the Church's prayer for you.

This cannot be done without facing up to the past, confronting the temptation of blaming circumstances or the other partner, and ridding yourself of self-justification. All breakdowns leave obligations behind them. The freedom that Christ wants for you is not a matter of ignoring these obligations, whether relational (e.g. in caring for your children) or economic. The Church's ministers are ready to help you engage in reflection and self-searching, if that is your wish, either in formal confession or in informal and exploratory discussion and prayer. The aim of this is to help you reach the truth that God desires to show you about your situation, not for anyone else to pass judgement.

The Church will welcome you into its worshipping fellowship, if you are not already part of it, as the essential resource for you to rebuild your life in the company of God and his people.

Appendix 2

The Church will advise you, as it advises those who have never been married, not to hurry into a new marriage. This advice needs to be carefully heeded, especially since mistakes and misjudgements made in the past can repeat themselves. If, after a serious length of time living alone and dealing responsibly with the legacy of the past marriage, you are certain that God has called you to a new one, the Church will pray with you and your new partner. The Service of Prayer and Dedication after a Civil Marriage is one way, widely available, in which it can do so formally. A marriage in church may currently be a possibility if you live in a parish where experimental diocesan guidelines are being followed. This presupposes, however, a serious willingness on your part to discuss the past honestly with the minister, and to allow him or her, in consultation with the bishop, the freedom to reach a decision about the appropriateness of your marrying in church.